REFA'S STORIES
The olive tree

Written and Illustrated by Ilaria Montalto

PREFACE

I was in my nursery courtyard which was full of olive trees and where we used to spend the afternoon playing. One afternoon, I was sitting under the shade of an olive tree with my legs crossed. I closed my eyes and found myself in midair, floating. I soared through the sky, overwhelmed with happiness and a sense of pride in my unique talent. Eager to share this extraordinary experience with my friends, I dashed towards them, urging them to gather around the olive tree and witness my grand display. But to my dismay, I was not able to fly again. In that moment, all I could envision were their mocking smiles and laughter.
Fortunately, it was just a dream. A recurring dream that I used to have when I was a child and that I still remember.

This dream became a significant topic during one of my therapy sessions. When my therapist asked me what I thought that dream meant, I told her that I believed it was the epitome of my social anxiety.

Social anxiety has been a constant companion in my life, silently shaping my interactions and leaving me feeling detached from others. Though, its presence was known to me only a couple of years ago when I embarked on my therapeutic journey, the feeling of being different and flawed had always lingered within me, defying explanation.

In recent years, a series of traumatic events, including the devastating impact of the pandemic, cast a dark shadow over my life. Depression, severe anxiety, and debilitating panic attacks further compounded my struggles, intensifying the grip of social anxiety.

These past years have been undeniably challenging, perhaps the most agonizing period of my life. Yet, amidst the turmoil, I made a resolute decision that my experience would not be relegated to a narrative of pure negativity. Instead, I sought to transform my pain into something purposeful, a catalyst for change.

I chose to craft a story, one that would illuminate the depths of metal health struggles and kindle compassion within those who read it. through this narrative, I aspire to raise awareness about the profound impact of mental health issues, eroding the stigma and fostering a greater understanding and empathy within society.

My journey is far from over, but I am determined to turn my scars into beacons of hope and resilience. Together, we can forge a path of healing and acceptance, embracing the beauty and complexity of the human experience, both its triumphs and its struggles.

P.s. Bear with me there might be more stories coming!

The olive tree

Once upon a time, in a small village nestled in the heart of the forest, there lived a young woman named Refa. She had big glasses and curly hair that seemed to have a life of its own. She was kind and clever, but there was a secret that she kept from the other villagers – she was a witch.

Refa had always known she was different from the other villagers, but she was afraid to reveal her true self. She kept her powers hidden and spent most of her days helping out at the local apothecary, using her knowledge of herb and plants to heal the sick and wounded.

One sunny day, Refa decided to take a break from her potion-making and gardening and spend some time under the shade of a massive olive tree. As she laid there, basking in the warmth of the sun, she closed her eyes and began to relax.

Suddenly, she felt a strange sensation, as if the ground beneath her was moving. She opened her eyes and was surprised to see that she was no longer lying on the ground but was floating in the air. She gasped in amazement as she realised that she could fly!

Refa was thrilled by her newfound ability, and she soared though the sky, admiring the village and the surrounding landscape from the top. She felt free and alive, and for the first time in her life, she felt truly powerful.

Filled with excitement, Refa flew back to the village. It was time to show to the entire village what she could do and what she was. She gathered all the villagers under the olive tree and announced that she had something incredible to show them. She told them about her secret, but the villagers started whispering between each other absolutely appalled by what she was saying.

Refa stood before the crowd, her heart pounding with excitement. She closed her eyes and focused all her energy on levitating into the air. She concentrated harder and harder, nut nothing seemed to happen.

After a few minutes of trying, Refa opened her eyes and realised that she was still standing on the ground. She looked around and saw that the villagers were laughing and pointing at her, mocking her failed attempt to impress them.

Feeling embarrassed and ashamed, Refa hung her head low and walked away from the crowd. She couldn't believe that she had failed in front of everyone and that her magic had let her down.

As she walked through the crowd, Refa heard whispers and snickers behind her back. The villagers had lost their respect for her, and they didn't seem to care that she was a kind and generous witch who had always used her magic knowledge for good.

Feeling alone and isolated, Refa retreated to her cottage on the edge of the forest. She spent days and nights alone, trying to figure out what had gone wrong and why her magic had failed her.

One night, as she laid awake in bed, she saw a beam of light coming through the window, she was immediately drawn to it. Without hesitation, she threw on her clothes and grabbed a lantern, heading outside to investigate.

As soon as she stepped out into the night, she saw that the beam of light had left a trail, leading deep into the forest. The light was like a magnet, drawing her forward, and Refa knew that she had to follow it. So she began to walk, her torch casting eerie shadows on the trees around her.

The trail was winding and difficult to follow, but Refa kept moving forward, her curiosity driving her on. After what felt like hours, she finally arrived at the entrance of a cave. The beam of light was coming from inside, and Refa knew that she had to go in.

As she entered the cave, she could feel her heart racing in her chest. The air was cold and damp, and the only sound was the echoing of her footsteps on the stone floor. The beam of light was now stronger than ever, and Refa followed it deeper into the cave.

Finally, she came to a large chamber, and in the centre of the room there was a crystal. The light was coming from it, and it was so brigh that Refa had to shield her eyes.

Suddenly, the crystal began to speak. Its voice was soft and soothing, and seemed to fill the entire chamber.

"Welcome, refa." Said the crystal. "I have been waiting for you."

Refa was stunned. She had never heard of a crystal that could speak before.

"I am the crystal of confidence." Said the crystal. "I have been watching you for some time, and I know about what happened under the olive tree."

Refa's heart sank.

"I can help you." Said the crystal. "But first, you must trust me."

Refa hesitated. She didn't know if she could trust a talking crystal but something inside her told her that she should listen.

"I will give you a gift." Said the crystal. "A gift of confidence. But in order to receive it, you must face your fears."

Refa felt a lump in her throat. She knew that facing her fears would be difficult, but she also knew that it was necessary.

"Take my gift" said the crystal "and go back to your village and face the other villagers and don't be afraid to show them your power."

Refa reached out and touched the crystal, and a warm glow spread through her body. She felt more confident than she ever had before.

With newfound courage, Refa left the cave and headed back towards her village. She was nervous, but she knew that she could face her fears.

As Refa arrived into the village she could feel the eyes of the villagers on her, but she held her head high and walked towards the olive tree.

For a moment Refa felt her courage falter. She could see the doubt in the villagers' eyes, the suspicion that she was completely crazy. But then she whispered to herself:

"I am a witch and I am proud of who I am. I believe in myself and my powers.

As Refa flew, she could feel the wind in her hair and the sun on her skin. She flew higher and higher until she could see the entire village beneath her. The villagers were watching in amazement as Refa soared through the sky.

She landed back on the ground and the villagers gathered around her. They were amazed and curious about how she could fly.

Refa explained that she had always knew of being a witch but she was afraid of how they might react. She told them about the beam of light that led her to the hidden cave where she found her courage.

The villagers listened in awe, and some of them even apologized for laughing at her before. They were now proud to have a witch among them, and they started to appreciate her differences.

From that day on, Refa was no longer alone. The villagers accepted her for who she was, and they were fascinated by her talent. They began to invite her to their celebrations and welcomed her into their homes.

Refa had finally found her place in the village, and she was no longer afraid to be herself. She knew that she was special, and that made her happy.

The End

To:

My parents, for supporting me throughout everything and for always believing in me.

Dario and Marinetta, for being present and sharing cat memes with me.

Monica, for always being there for me, through thick and thin!

All the people that have been part of my journey and to the one that decided to leave.

And of course, to myself.